Agile and Scrum Foundations

Experience Agile and Scrum in two days

Richard Kasperowski

—— WITH GREAT PEOPLE ——

High-Performance Teams l Core Protocols l Agile l Open Space Technology
+1 617 466 9754 l richard@kasperowski.com l kasperowski.com l @rkasper

Richard Kasperowski | With Great People

Richard Kasperowski is an author, speaker, teacher, and coach focused on high-performance teams. Richard is the author of the new book, *High-Performance Teams: The Foundations*, as well as *The Core Protocols: A Guide to Greatness*. He leads clients in building and maintaining high-performance teams that get great results using the Core Protocols, Agile, and Open Space Technology. Richard created and teaches the course Agile Software Development at Harvard University. Learn more and subscribe to Richard's newsletter at kasperowski.com.

Course Backlog

✓Set up

✓Introduction to the Course

✓Introduction to Agile

✓Scrum

✓Agile Requirements

✓Definition of Done, Definition of Ready

✓Estimating

✓Agile Forecasting & Project Management

✓Sprint Planning

✓Retrospectives

✓Class Project

✓Next Steps

✓Clean Up

Introduction to the course

Your notes & key take-aways:

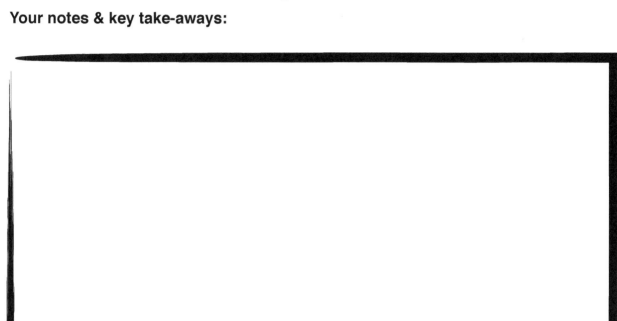

Introduction to Agile

Manifesto for Agile Software Development

We are uncovering better ways of developing software by doing it and helping others do it. Through this work we have come to value:

Individuals and interactions over processes and tools

Working software over comprehensive documentation

Customer collaboration over contract negotiation

Responding to change over following a plan

That is, while there is value in the items on the right, we value the items on the left more.

Richard Kasperowski I High-Performance Teams I Core Protocols I Agile I Open Space Technology
+1 617 466 9754 I richard@kasperowski.com I kasperowski.com

- 3 -

Principles behind the Agile Manifesto

We follow these principles:

Our highest priority is to satisfy the customer through early and continuous delivery of valuable software.

Welcome changing requirements, even late in development. Agile processes harness change for the customer's competitive advantage.

Deliver working software frequently, from a couple of weeks to a couple of months, with a preference to the shorter timescale.

Business people and developers must work together daily throughout the project.

Build projects around motivated individuals. Give them the environment and support they need, and trust them to get the job done.

The most efficient and effective method of conveying information to and within a development team is face-to-face conversation.

Working software is the primary measure of progress.

Agile processes promote sustainable development. The sponsors, developers, and users should be able to maintain a constant pace indefinitely.

Continuous attention to technical excellence and good design enhances agility.

Simplicity--the art of maximizing the amount of work not done--is essential.

The best architectures, requirements, and designs emerge from self-organizing teams.

At regular intervals, the team reflects on how to become more effective, then tunes and adjusts its behavior accordingly.

[agilemanifesto.org, accessed 2017-10-23]

Your notes & key take-aways:

Richard Kasperowski | High-Performance Teams | Core Protocols | Agile | Open Space Technology
+1 617 466 9754 | richard@kasperowski.com | kasperowski.com

- 4 -

Scrum

The Scrum Guide™

This HTML version of the Scrum Guide is a direct port of the November 2017 version available as a PDF here.

Purpose of the Scrum Guide

Scrum is a framework for developing, delivering, and sustaining complex products. This Guide contains the definition of Scrum. This definition consists of Scrum's roles, events, artifacts, and the rules that bind them together. Ken Schwaber and Jeff Sutherland developed Scrum; the Scrum Guide is written and provided by them. Together, they stand behind the Scrum Guide.

Definition of Scrum

Scrum (n): A framework within which people can address complex adaptive problems, while productively and creatively delivering products of the highest possible value.

Scrum is:

- Lightweight
- Simple to understand
- Difficult to master

Scrum is a process framework that has been used to manage work on complex products since the early 1990s. Scrum is not a process, technique, or definitive method. Rather, it is a framework within which you can employ various processes and techniques. Scrum makes clear the relative efficacy of your product management and work techniques so that you can continuously improve the product, the team, and the working environment.

The Scrum framework consists of Scrum Teams and their associated roles, events, artifacts, and rules. Each component within the framework serves a specific purpose and is essential to Scrum's success and usage.

The rules of Scrum bind together the roles, events, and artifacts, governing the relationships and interaction between them. The rules of Scrum are described throughout the body of this document.

Specific tactics for using the Scrum framework vary and are described elsewhere.

Uses of Scrum

Scrum was initially developed for managing and developing products. Starting in the early 1990s, Scrum has been used extensively, worldwide, to:

Richard Kasperowski | High-Performance Teams | Core Protocols | Agile | Open Space Technology
+1 617 466 9754 | richard@kasperowski.com | kasperowski.com

- 5 -

1. Research and identify viable markets, technologies, and product capabilities;

2. Develop products and enhancements;

3. Release products and enhancements, as frequently as many times per day;

4. Develop and sustain Cloud (online, secure, on-demand) and other operational environments for product use; and,

5. Sustain and renew products.

Scrum has been used to develop software, hardware, embedded software, networks of interacting function, autonomous vehicles, schools, government, marketing, managing the operation of organizations and almost everything we use in our daily lives, as individuals and societies.

As technology, market, and environmental complexities and their interactions have rapidly increased, Scrum's utility in dealing with complexity is proven daily.

Scrum proved especially effective in iterative and incremental knowledge transfer. Scrum is now widely used for products, services, and the management of the parent organization.

The essence of Scrum is a small team of people. The individual team is highly flexible and adaptive. These strengths continue operating in single, several, many, and networks of teams that develop, release, operate and sustain the work and work products of thousands of people. They collaborate and interoperate through sophisticated development architectures and target release environments.

When the words "develop" and "development" are used in the Scrum Guide, they refer to complex work, such as those types identified above.

Scrum Theory

Scrum is founded on empirical process control theory, or empiricism. Empiricism asserts that knowledge comes from experience and making decisions based on what is known. Scrum employs an iterative, incremental approach to optimize predictability and control risk. Three pillars uphold every implementation of empirical process control: transparency, inspection, and adaptation.

Transparency

Significant aspects of the process must be visible to those responsible for the outcome. Transparency requires those aspects be defined by a common standard so observers share a common understanding of what is being seen.

For example:

A common language referring to the process must be shared by all participants; and,

Richard Kasperowski | High-Performance Teams | Core Protocols | Agile | Open Space Technology
+1 617 466 9754 | richard@kasperowski.com | kasperowski.com

- 6 -

Those performing the work and those inspecting the resulting increment must share a common definition of "Done".

Inspection

Scrum users must frequently inspect Scrum artifacts and progress toward a Sprint Goal to detect undesirable variances. Their inspection should not be so frequent that inspection gets in the way of the work. Inspections are most beneficial when diligently performed by skilled inspectors at the point of work.

Adaptation

If an inspector determines that one or more aspects of a process deviate outside acceptable limits, and that the resulting product will be unacceptable, the process or the material being processed must be adjusted. An adjustment must be made as soon as possible to minimize further deviation.

Scrum prescribes four formal events for inspection and adaptation, as described in the Scrum Events section of this document:

- Sprint Planning
- Daily Scrum
- Sprint Review
- Sprint Retrospective

Scrum Values

When the values of commitment, courage, focus, openness and respect are embodied and lived by the Scrum Team, the Scrum pillars of transparency, inspection, and adaptation come to life and build trust for everyone. The Scrum Team members learn and explore those values as they work with the Scrum events, roles and artifacts.

Successful use of Scrum depends on people becoming more proficient in living these five values. People personally commit to achieving the goals of the Scrum Team. The Scrum Team members have courage to do the right thing and work on tough problems. Everyone focuses on the work of the Sprint and the goals of the Scrum Team. The Scrum Team and its stakeholders agree to be open about all the work and the challenges with performing the work. Scrum Team members respect each other to be capable, independent people.

The Scrum Team

The Scrum Team consists of a Product Owner, the Development Team, and a Scrum Master. Scrum Teams are self-organizing and cross-functional. Self-organizing teams choose how best to accomplish their work, rather than being directed by others outside the team. Cross-functional teams have all competencies needed to accomplish the work

Richard Kasperowski I High-Performance Teams I Core Protocols I Agile I Open Space Technology
+1 617 466 9754 I richard@kasperowski.com I kasperowski.com

- 7 -

without depending on others not part of the team. The team model in Scrum is designed to optimize flexibility, creativity, and productivity. The Scrum Team has proven itself to be increasingly effective for all the earlier stated uses, and any complex work.

Scrum Teams deliver products iteratively and incrementally, maximizing opportunities for feedback. Incremental deliveries of "Done" product ensure a potentially useful version of working product is always available.

The Product Owner

The Product Owner is responsible for maximizing the value of the product resulting from work of the Development Team. How this is done may vary widely across organizations, Scrum Teams, and individuals.

The Product Owner is the sole person responsible for managing the Product Backlog. Product Backlog management includes:

- Clearly expressing Product Backlog items;

- Ordering the items in the Product Backlog to best achieve goals and missions;

- Optimizing the value of the work the Development Team performs;

- Ensuring that the Product Backlog is visible, transparent, and clear to all, and shows what the Scrum Team will work on next; and,

- Ensuring the Development Team understands items in the Product Backlog to the level needed.

The Product Owner may do the above work, or have the Development Team do it. However, the Product Owner remains accountable.

The Product Owner is one person, not a committee. The Product Owner may represent the desires of a committee in the Product Backlog, but those wanting to change a Product Backlog item's priority must address the Product Owner.

For the Product Owner to succeed, the entire organization must respect his or her decisions. The Product Owner's decisions are visible in the content and ordering of the Product Backlog. No one can force the Development Team to work from a different set of requirements.

The Development Team

The Development Team consists of professionals who do the work of delivering a potentially releasable Increment of "Done" product at the end of each Sprint. A "Done" increment is required at the Sprint Review. Only members of the Development Team create the Increment.

Richard Kasperowski | High-Performance Teams | Core Protocols | Agile | Open Space Technology
+1 617 466 9754 | richard@kasperowski.com | kasperowski.com

- 8 -

Development Teams are structured and empowered by the organization to organize and manage their own work. The resulting synergy optimizes the Development Team's overall efficiency and effectiveness.

Development Teams have the following characteristics:

They are self-organizing. No one (not even the Scrum Master) tells the Development Team how to turn Product Backlog into Increments of potentially releasable functionality;

Development Teams are cross-functional, with all the skills as a team necessary to create a product Increment;

Scrum recognizes no titles for Development Team members, regardless of the work being performed by the person;

Scrum recognizes no sub-teams in the Development Team, regardless of domains that need to be addressed like testing, architecture, operations, or business analysis; and,

Individual Development Team members may have specialized skills and areas of focus, but accountability belongs to the Development Team as a whole.

Development Team Size

Optimal Development Team size is small enough to remain nimble and large enough to complete significant work within a Sprint. Fewer than three Development Team members decrease interaction and results in smaller productivity gains. Smaller Development Teams may encounter skill constraints during the Sprint, causing the Development Team to be unable to deliver a potentially releasable Increment. Having more than nine members requires too much coordination. Large Development Teams generate too much complexity for an empirical process to be useful. The Product Owner and Scrum Master roles are not included in this count unless they are also executing the work of the Sprint Backlog.

The Scrum Master

The Scrum Master is responsible for promoting and supporting Scrum as defined in the Scrum Guide. Scrum Masters do this by helping everyone understand Scrum theory, practices, rules, and values.

The Scrum Master is a servant-leader for the Scrum Team. The Scrum Master helps those outside the Scrum Team understand which of their interactions with the Scrum Team are helpful and which aren't. The Scrum Master helps everyone change these interactions to maximize the value created by the Scrum Team.

Scrum Master Service to the Product Owner

The Scrum Master serves the Product Owner in several ways, including:

Richard Kasperowski | High-Performance Teams | Core Protocols | Agile | Open Space Technology
+1 617 466 9754 | richard@kasperowski.com | kasperowski.com

- 9 -

- Ensuring that goals, scope, and product domain are understood by everyone on the Scrum Team as well as possible;

- Finding techniques for effective Product Backlog management;

- Helping the Scrum Team understand the need for clear and concise Product Backlog items;

- Understanding product planning in an empirical environment;

- Ensuring the Product Owner knows how to arrange the Product Backlog to maximize value;

- Understanding and practicing agility; and,

- Facilitating Scrum events as requested or needed.

Scrum Master Service to the Development Team

The Scrum Master serves the Development Team in several ways, including:

- Coaching the Development Team in self-organization and cross-functionality;

- Helping the Development Team to create high-value products;

- Removing impediments to the Development Team's progress;

- Facilitating Scrum events as requested or needed; and,

- Coaching the Development Team in organizational environments in which Scrum is not yet fully adopted and understood.

Scrum Master Service to the Organization

- The Scrum Master serves the organization in several ways, including:

- Leading and coaching the organization in its Scrum adoption;

- Planning Scrum implementations within the organization;

- Helping employees and stakeholders understand and enact Scrum and empirical product development;

- Causing change that increases the productivity of the Scrum Team; and,

- Working with other Scrum Masters to increase the effectiveness of the application of Scrum in the organization.

Scrum Events

Prescribed events are used in Scrum to create regularity and to minimize the need for meetings not defined in Scrum. All events are time-boxed events, such that every event

Richard Kasperowski | High-Performance Teams | Core Protocols | Agile | Open Space Technology
+1 617 466 9754 | richard@kasperowski.com | kasperowski.com

- 10 -

has a maximum duration. Once a Sprint begins, its duration is fixed and cannot be shortened or lengthened. The remaining events may end whenever the purpose of the event is achieved, ensuring an appropriate amount of time is spent without allowing waste in the process.

Other than the Sprint itself, which is a container for all other events, each event in Scrum is a formal opportunity to inspect and adapt something. These events are specifically designed to enable critical transparency and inspection. Failure to include any of these events results in reduced transparency and is a lost opportunity to inspect and adapt.

The Sprint

The heart of Scrum is a Sprint, a time-box of one month or less during which a "Done", useable, and potentially releasable product Increment is created. Sprints have consistent durations throughout a development effort. A new Sprint starts immediately after the conclusion of the previous Sprint.

Sprints contain and consist of the Sprint Planning, Daily Scrums, the development work, the Sprint Review, and the Sprint Retrospective.

During the Sprint:

No changes are made that would endanger the Sprint Goal;

Quality goals do not decrease; and,

Scope may be clarified and re-negotiated between the Product Owner and Development Team as more is learned.

Each Sprint may be considered a project with no more than a one-month horizon. Like projects, Sprints are used to accomplish something. Each Sprint has a goal of what is to be built, a design and flexible plan that will guide building it, the work, and the resultant product increment.

Sprints are limited to one calendar month. When a Sprint's horizon is too long the definition of what is being built may change, complexity may rise, and risk may increase. Sprints enable predictability by ensuring inspection and adaptation of progress toward a Sprint Goal at least every calendar month. Sprints also limit risk to one calendar month of cost.

Cancelling a Sprint

A Sprint can be cancelled before the Sprint time-box is over. Only the Product Owner has the authority to cancel the Sprint, although he or she may do so under influence from the stakeholders, the Development Team, or the Scrum Master.

Richard Kasperowski I High-Performance Teams I Core Protocols I Agile I Open Space Technology
+1 617 466 9754 I richard@kasperowski.com I kasperowski.com

- 11 -

A Sprint would be cancelled if the Sprint Goal becomes obsolete. This might occur if the company changes direction or if market or technology conditions change. In general, a Sprint should be cancelled if it no longer makes sense given the circumstances. But, due to the short duration of Sprints, cancellation rarely makes sense.

When a Sprint is cancelled, any completed and "Done" Product Backlog items are reviewed. If part of the work is potentially releasable, the Product Owner typically accepts it. All incomplete Product Backlog Items are re-estimated and put back on the Product Backlog. The work done on them depreciates quickly and must be frequently re-estimated.

Sprint cancellations consume resources, since everyone regroups in another Sprint Planning to start another Sprint. Sprint cancellations are often traumatic to the Scrum Team, and are very uncommon.

Sprint Planning

The work to be performed in the Sprint is planned at the Sprint Planning. This plan is created by the collaborative work of the entire Scrum Team.

Sprint Planning is time-boxed to a maximum of eight hours for a one-month Sprint. For shorter Sprints, the event is usually shorter. The Scrum Master ensures that the event takes place and that attendants understand its purpose. The Scrum Master teaches the Scrum Team to keep it within the time-box.

Sprint Planning answers the following:

- What can be delivered in the Increment resulting from the upcoming Sprint?

- How will the work needed to deliver the Increment be achieved?

Topic One: What can be done this Sprint?

The Development Team works to forecast the functionality that will be developed during the Sprint. The Product Owner discusses the objective that the Sprint should achieve and the Product Backlog items that, if completed in the Sprint, would achieve the Sprint Goal. The entire Scrum Team collaborates on understanding the work of the Sprint.

The input to this meeting is the Product Backlog, the latest product Increment, projected capacity of the Development Team during the Sprint, and past performance of the Development Team. The number of items selected from the Product Backlog for the Sprint is solely up to the Development Team. Only the Development Team can assess what it can accomplish over the upcoming Sprint.

During Sprint Planning the Scrum Team also crafts a Sprint Goal. The Sprint Goal is an objective that will be met within the Sprint through the implementation of the Product Backlog, and it provides guidance to the Development Team on why it is building the Increment.

Richard Kasperowski I High-Performance Teams I Core Protocols I Agile I Open Space Technology
+1 617 466 9754 I richard@kasperowski.com I kasperowski.com

- 12 -

Having set the Sprint Goal and selected the Product Backlog items for the Sprint, the Development Team decides how it will build this functionality into a "Done" product Increment during the Sprint. The Product Backlog items selected for this Sprint plus the plan for delivering them is called the Sprint Backlog.

The Development Team usually starts by designing the system and the work needed to convert the Product Backlog into a working product Increment. Work may be of varying size, or estimated effort. However, enough work is planned during Sprint Planning for the Development Team to forecast what it believes it can do in the upcoming Sprint. Work planned for the first days of the Sprint by the Development Team is decomposed by the end of this meeting, often to units of one day or less. The Development Team self-organizes to undertake the work in the Sprint Backlog, both during Sprint Planning and as needed throughout the Sprint.

The Product Owner can help to clarify the selected Product Backlog items and make trade-offs. If the Development Team determines it has too much or too little work, it may renegotiate the selected Product Backlog items with the Product Owner. The Development Team may also invite other people to attend to provide technical or domain advice.

By the end of the Sprint Planning, the Development Team should be able to explain to the Product Owner and Scrum Master how it intends to work as a self-organizing team to accomplish the Sprint Goal and create the anticipated Increment.

Sprint Goal

The Sprint Goal is an objective set for the Sprint that can be met through the implementation of Product Backlog. It provides guidance to the Development Team on why it is building the Increment. It is created during the Sprint Planning meeting. The Sprint Goal gives the Development Team some flexibility regarding the functionality implemented within the Sprint. The selected Product Backlog items deliver one coherent function, which can be the Sprint Goal. The Sprint Goal can be any other coherence that causes the Development Team to work together rather than on separate initiatives.

As the Development Team works, it keeps the Sprint Goal in mind. In order to satisfy the Sprint Goal, it implements functionality and technology. If the work turns out to be different than the Development Team expected, they collaborate with the Product Owner to negotiate the scope of Sprint Backlog within the Sprint.

Daily Scrum

The Daily Scrum is a 15-minute time-boxed event for the Development Team. The Daily Scrum is held every day of the Sprint. At it, the Development Team plans work for the next 24 hours. This optimizes team collaboration and performance by inspecting the

Richard Kasperowski I High-Performance Teams I Core Protocols I Agile I Open Space Technology
+1 617 466 9754 I richard@kasperowski.com I kasperowski.com

- 13 -

work since the last Daily Scrum and forecasting upcoming Sprint work. The Daily Scrum is held at the same time and place each day to reduce complexity.

The Development Team uses the Daily Scrum to inspect progress toward the Sprint Goal and to inspect how progress is trending toward completing the work in the Sprint Backlog. The Daily Scrum optimizes the probability that the Development Team will meet the Sprint Goal. Every day, the Development Team should understand how it intends to work together as a self-organizing team to accomplish the Sprint Goal and create the anticipated Increment by the end of the Sprint.

The structure of the meeting is set by the Development Team and can be conducted in different ways if it focuses on progress toward the Sprint Goal. Some Development Teams will use questions, some will be more discussion based. Here is an example of what might be used:

- What did I do yesterday that helped the Development Team meet the Sprint Goal?

- What will I do today to help the Development Team meet the Sprint Goal?

- Do I see any impediment that prevents me or the Development Team from meeting the Sprint Goal?

The Development Team or team members often meet immediately after the Daily Scrum for detailed discussions, or to adapt, or replan, the rest of the Sprint's work.

The Scrum Master ensures that the Development Team has the meeting, but the Development Team is responsible for conducting the Daily Scrum. The Scrum Master teaches the Development Team to keep the Daily Scrum within the 15-minute time-box.

The Daily Scrum is an internal meeting for the Development Team. If others are present, the Scrum Master ensures that they do not disrupt the meeting.

Daily Scrums improve communications, eliminate other meetings, identify impediments to development for removal, highlight and promote quick decision-making, and improve the Development Team's level of knowledge. This is a key inspect and adapt meeting.

Sprint Review

A Sprint Review is held at the end of the Sprint to inspect the Increment and adapt the Product Backlog if needed. During the Sprint Review, the Scrum Team and stakeholders collaborate about what was done in the Sprint. Based on that and any changes to the Product Backlog during the Sprint, attendees collaborate on the next things that could be done to optimize value. This is an informal meeting, not a status meeting, and the presentation of the Increment is intended to elicit feedback and foster collaboration.

This is at most a four-hour meeting for one-month Sprints. For shorter Sprints, the event is usually shorter. The Scrum Master ensures that the event takes place and that

Richard Kasperowski | High-Performance Teams | Core Protocols | Agile | Open Space Technology
+1 617 466 9754 | richard@kasperowski.com | kasperowski.com

- 14 -

attendees understand its purpose. The Scrum Master teaches everyone involved to keep it within the time-box.

The Sprint Review includes the following elements:

- Attendees include the Scrum Team and key stakeholders invited by the Product Owner;

- The Product Owner explains what Product Backlog items have been "Done" and what has not been "Done";

- The Development Team discusses what went well during the Sprint, what problems it ran into, and how those problems were solved;

- The Development Team demonstrates the work that it has "Done" and answers questions about the Increment;

- The Product Owner discusses the Product Backlog as it stands. He or she projects likely target and delivery dates based on progress to date (if needed);

- The entire group collaborates on what to do next, so that the Sprint Review provides valuable input to subsequent Sprint Planning;

- Review of how the marketplace or potential use of the product might have changed what is the most valuable thing to do next; and,

- Review of the timeline, budget, potential capabilities, and marketplace for the next anticipated releases of functionality or capability of the product.

The result of the Sprint Review is a revised Product Backlog that defines the probable Product Backlog items for the next Sprint. The Product Backlog may also be adjusted overall to meet new opportunities.

Sprint Retrospective

The Sprint Retrospective is an opportunity for the Scrum Team to inspect itself and create a plan for improvements to be enacted during the next Sprint.

The Sprint Retrospective occurs after the Sprint Review and prior to the next Sprint Planning. This is at most a three-hour meeting for one-month Sprints. For shorter Sprints, the event is usually shorter. The Scrum Master ensures that the event takes place and that attendants understand its purpose.

The Scrum Master ensures that the meeting is positive and productive. The Scrum Master teaches all to keep it within the time-box. The Scrum Master participates as a peer team member in the meeting from the accountability over the Scrum process.

The purpose of the Sprint Retrospective is to:

Richard Kasperowski | High-Performance Teams | Core Protocols | Agile | Open Space Technology
+1 617 466 9754 | richard@kasperowski.com | kasperowski.com

- 15 -

- Inspect how the last Sprint went with regards to people, relationships, process, and tools;

- Identify and order the major items that went well and potential improvements; and,

- Create a plan for implementing improvements to the way the Scrum Team does its work.

The Scrum Master encourages the Scrum Team to improve, within the Scrum process framework, its development process and practices to make it more effective and enjoyable for the next Sprint. During each Sprint Retrospective, the Scrum Team plans ways to increase product quality by improving work processes or adapting the definition of "Done", if appropriate and not in conflict with product or organizational standards.

By the end of the Sprint Retrospective, the Scrum Team should have identified improvements that it will implement in the next Sprint. Implementing these improvements in the next Sprint is the adaptation to the inspection of the Scrum Team itself. Although improvements may be implemented at any time, the Sprint Retrospective provides a formal opportunity to focus on inspection and adaptation.

Scrum Artifacts

Scrum's artifacts represent work or value to provide transparency and opportunities for inspection and adaptation. Artifacts defined by Scrum are specifically designed to maximize transparency of key information so that everybody has the same understanding of the artifact.

Product Backlog

The Product Backlog is an ordered list of everything that is known to be needed in the product. It is the single source of requirements for any changes to be made to the product. The Product Owner is responsible for the Product Backlog, including its content, availability, and ordering.

A Product Backlog is never complete. The earliest development of it lays out the initially known and best-understood requirements. The Product Backlog evolves as the product and the environment in which it will be used evolves. The Product Backlog is dynamic; it constantly changes to identify what the product needs to be appropriate, competitive, and useful. If a product exists, its Product Backlog also exists.

The Product Backlog lists all features, functions, requirements, enhancements, and fixes that constitute the changes to be made to the product in future releases. Product Backlog items have the attributes of a description, order, estimate, and value. Product Backlog items often include test descriptions that will prove its completeness when "Done".

As a product is used and gains value, and the marketplace provides feedback, the Product Backlog becomes a larger and more exhaustive list. Requirements never stop

Richard Kasperowski | High-Performance Teams | Core Protocols | Agile | Open Space Technology
+1 617 466 9754 | richard@kasperowski.com | kasperowski.com

changing, so a Product Backlog is a living artifact. Changes in business requirements, market conditions, or technology may cause changes in the Product Backlog.

Multiple Scrum Teams often work together on the same product. One Product Backlog is used to describe the upcoming work on the product. A Product Backlog attribute that groups items may then be employed.

Product Backlog refinement is the act of adding detail, estimates, and order to items in the Product Backlog. This is an ongoing process in which the Product Owner and the Development Team collaborate on the details of Product Backlog items. During Product Backlog refinement, items are reviewed and revised. The Scrum Team decides how and when refinement is done. Refinement usually consumes no more than 10% of the capacity of the Development Team. However, Product Backlog items can be updated at any time by the Product Owner or at the Product Owner's discretion.

Higher ordered Product Backlog items are usually clearer and more detailed than lower ordered ones. More precise estimates are made based on the greater clarity and increased detail; the lower the order, the less detail. Product Backlog items that will occupy the Development Team for the upcoming Sprint are refined so that any one item can reasonably be "Done" within the Sprint time-box. Product Backlog items that can be "Done" by the Development Team within one Sprint are deemed "Ready" for selection in a Sprint Planning. Product Backlog items usually acquire this degree of transparency through the above described refining activities.

The Development Team is responsible for all estimates. The Product Owner may influence the Development Team by helping it understand and select trade-offs, but the people who will perform the work make the final estimate.

Monitoring Progress Toward Goals

At any point in time, the total work remaining to reach a goal can be summed. The Product Owner tracks this total work remaining at least every Sprint Review. The Product Owner compares this amount with work remaining at previous Sprint Reviews to assess progress toward completing projected work by the desired time for the goal. This information is made transparent to all stakeholders.

Various projective practices upon trending have been used to forecast progress, like burn-downs, burn-ups, or cumulative flows. These have proven useful. However, these do not replace the importance of empiricism. In complex environments, what will happen is unknown. Only what has already happened may be used for forward-looking decision-making.

Sprint Backlog

The Sprint Backlog is the set of Product Backlog items selected for the Sprint, plus a plan for delivering the product Increment and realizing the Sprint Goal. The Sprint Backlog is a forecast by the Development Team about what functionality will be in the

Richard Kasperowski | High-Performance Teams | Core Protocols | Agile | Open Space Technology
+1 617 466 9754 | richard@kasperowski.com | kasperowski.com

- 17 -

next Increment and the work needed to deliver that functionality into a "Done" Increment.

The Sprint Backlog makes visible all the work that the Development Team identifies as necessary to meet the Sprint Goal. To ensure continuous improvement, it includes at least one high priority process improvement identified in the previous Retrospective meeting.

The Sprint Backlog is a plan with enough detail that changes in progress can be understood in the Daily Scrum. The Development Team modifies the Sprint Backlog throughout the Sprint, and the Sprint Backlog emerges during the Sprint. This emergence occurs as the Development Team works through the plan and learns more about the work needed to achieve the Sprint Goal.

As new work is required, the Development Team adds it to the Sprint Backlog. As work is performed or completed, the estimated remaining work is updated. When elements of the plan are deemed unnecessary, they are removed. Only the Development Team can change its Sprint Backlog during a Sprint. The Sprint Backlog is a highly visible, real-time picture of the work that the Development Team plans to accomplish during the Sprint, and it belongs solely to the Development Team.

Monitoring Sprint Progress

At any point in time in a Sprint, the total work remaining in the Sprint Backlog can be summed. The Development Team tracks this total work remaining at least for every Daily Scrum to project the likelihood of achieving the Sprint Goal. By tracking the remaining work throughout the Sprint, the Development Team can manage its progress.

Increment

The Increment is the sum of all the Product Backlog items completed during a Sprint and the value of the increments of all previous Sprints. At the end of a Sprint, the new Increment must be "Done," which means it must be in useable condition and meet the Scrum Team's definition of "Done". An increment is a body of inspectable, done work that supports empiricism at the end of the Sprint. The increment is a step toward a vision or goal. The increment must be in useable condition regardless of whether the Product Owner decides to release it.

Artifact Transparency

Scrum relies on transparency. Decisions to optimize value and control risk are made based on the perceived state of the artifacts. To the extent that transparency is complete, these decisions have a sound basis. To the extent that the artifacts are incompletely transparent, these decisions can be flawed, value may diminish and risk may increase.

Richard Kasperowski | High-Performance Teams | Core Protocols | Agile | Open Space Technology
+1 617 466 9754 | richard@kasperowski.com | kasperowski.com

- 18 -

The Scrum Master must work with the Product Owner, Development Team, and other involved parties to understand if the artifacts are completely transparent. There are practices for coping with incomplete transparency; the Scrum Master must help everyone apply the most appropriate practices in the absence of complete transparency. A Scrum Master can detect incomplete transparency by inspecting the artifacts, sensing patterns, listening closely to what is being said, and detecting differences between expected and real results.

The Scrum Master's job is to work with the Scrum Team and the organization to increase the transparency of the artifacts. This work usually involves learning, convincing, and change. Transparency doesn't occur overnight, but is a path.

Definition of "Done"

When a Product Backlog item or an Increment is described as "Done", everyone must understand what "Done" means. Although this may vary significantly per Scrum Team, members must have a shared understanding of what it means for work to be complete, to ensure transparency. This is the definition of "Done" for the Scrum Team and is used to assess when work is complete on the product Increment.

The same definition guides the Development Team in knowing how many Product Backlog items it can select during a Sprint Planning. The purpose of each Sprint is to deliver Increments of potentially releasable functionality that adhere to the Scrum Team's current definition of "Done".

Development Teams deliver an Increment of product functionality every Sprint. This Increment is useable, so a Product Owner may choose to immediately release it. If the definition of "Done" for an increment is part of the conventions, standards or guidelines of the development organization, all Scrum Teams must follow it as a minimum.

If "Done" for an increment is not a convention of the development organization, the Development Team of the Scrum Team must define a definition of "Done" appropriate for the product. If there are multiple Scrum Teams working on the system or product release, the Development Teams on all the Scrum Teams must mutually define the definition of "Done".

Each Increment is additive to all prior Increments and thoroughly tested, ensuring that all Increments work together.

As Scrum Teams mature, it is expected that their definitions of "Done" will expand to include more stringent criteria for higher quality. New definitions, as used, may uncover work to be done in previously "Done" increments. Any one product or system should have a definition of "Done" that is a standard for any work done on it.

End Note

Scrum is free and offered in this Guide. Scrum's roles, events, artifacts, and rules are immutable and although implementing only parts of Scrum is possible, the result is not

Richard Kasperowski I High-Performance Teams I Core Protocols I Agile I Open Space Technology
+1 617 466 9754 I richard@kasperowski.com I kasperowski.com

- 19 -

Scrum. Scrum exists only in its entirety and functions well as a container for other techniques, methodologies, and practices.

Acknowledgements

People

Of the thousands of people who have contributed to Scrum, we should single out those who were instrumental at the start: Jeff Sutherland worked with Jeff McKenna and John Scumniotales, and Ken Schwaber worked with Mike Smith and Chris Martin, and all of them worked together. Many others contributed in the ensuing years and without their help Scrum would not be refined as it is today.

History

Ken Schwaber and Jeff Sutherland worked on Scrum until 1995, when they co-presented Scrum at the OOPSLA Conference in 1995. This presentation essentially documented the learning that Ken and Jeff gained over the previous few years, and made public the first formal definition of Scrum.

The history of Scrum is described elsewhere. To honor the first places where it was tried and refined, we recognize Individual, Inc., Newspage, Fidelity Investments, and IDX (now GE Health).

The Scrum Guide documents Scrum as developed, evolved, and sustained for 20-plus years by Jeff Sutherland and Ken Schwaber. Other sources provide you with patterns, processes, and insights that complement the Scrum framework. These may increase productivity, value, creativity, and satisfaction with the results.

©2018 Ken Schwaber and Jeff Sutherland. Offered for license under the Attribution Share-Alike license of Creative Commons, accessible at http://creativecommons.org/licenses/by-sa/4.0/legalcode and also described in summary form at http://creativecommons.org/licenses/by-sa/4.0/. By utilizing this Scrum Guide you acknowledge and agree that you have read and agree to be bound by the terms of the Attribution ShareAlike license of Creative Commons.

[scrumguides.org, retrieved 2018-09-20]

Richard Kasperowski I High-Performance Teams I Core Protocols I Agile I Open Space Technology
+1 617 466 9754 I richard@kasperowski.com I kasperowski.com

- 20 -

Your notes & key take-aways:

Richard Kasperowski | High-Performance Teams | Core Protocols | Agile | Open Space Technology
+1 617 466 9754 | richard@kasperowski.com | kasperowski.com

- 21 -

Agile Requirements

Your notes & key take-aways:

Definition of Done, Definition of Ready

Your notes & key take-aways:

Richard Kasperowski I High-Performance Teams I Core Protocols I Agile I Open Space Technology
+1 617 466 9754 I richard@kasperowski.com I kasperowski.com

- 22 -

Estimating

Your notes & key take-aways:

Agile Forecasting & Project Management

Your notes & key take-aways:

Richard Kasperowski | High-Performance Teams | Core Protocols | Agile | Open Space Technology
+1 617 466 9754 | richard@kasperowski.com | kasperowski.com

- 23 -

Sprint Planning

Your notes & key take-aways:

Retrospectives

Your notes & key take-aways:

Richard Kasperowski I High-Performance Teams I Core Protocols I Agile I Open Space Technology
+1 617 466 9754 I richard@kasperowski.com I kasperowski.com

- 24 -

class Project

Your notes & key take-aways:

Next Steps

Your next steps:

Richard Kasperowski I High-Performance Teams I Core Protocols I Agile I Open Space Technology
+1 617 466 9754 I richard@kasperowski.com I kasperowski.com

- 25 -

Richard Kasperowski | High-Performance Teams | Core Protocols | Agile | Open Space Technology
+1 617 466 9754 | richard@kasperowski.com | kasperowski.com

- 26 -

Richard Kasperowski

—— WITH GREAT PEOPLE ——

www.ingramcontent.com/pod-product-compliance
Lightning Source LLC
Chambersburg PA
CBHW08054506036
40690CB00022B/5228